Is It Better to be Judged by a Jury of Your Peers Than by a Judge?

Caroline Leavitt

MONDO

For Jeff and Max, with love
—C.L.

Text copyright © 2007 by Caroline Leavitt

Photo credits:

YES! Cover: © Royalty-Free/Corbis; p. 4: Britt Erlanson/The Image Bank/Getty Images; p. 6: Hulton Archive/Getty Images; p. 7: © Associated Press, AP; p. 8: Sigrid Olsson/The Image Bank/Getty Images; p. 9: Graeme Robertson/Reportage/Getty Images; p. 10: Stockbyte Platinum/Getty Images; p. 12: David Young-Wolff/Stone/Getty Images; p. 13: © Matthew Cavanaugh/epa/Corbis; p. 15: © Reuters/CORBIS; p. 16: © Bettmann/CORBIS; p. 17: Picture Press/Photonica/Getty Images; p. 18: Jim Arbogast/Digital Vision/Getty Images; p. 19: Martin Barraud/Stone +/Getty Images; p. 20: Michael Kelley/Stone/Getty Images

NO! Cover: © Royalty-Free/Corbis; p. 4: © John Gress/Reuters/Corbis; p. 8: © Royalty-Free/Corbis; p. 9: Nicholas Eveleigh/Iconica/Getty Images; p. 11: Jim Arbogast/Digital Vision/Getty Images; p. 12: © Associated Press, POOL THE WASHINGTON POST; p. 13: © Dennis Cooper/zefa/Corbis; p. 14: © Royalty-Free/Corbis; p. 15: © Jon Feingersh/zefa/Corbis; p. 18: © Royalty-Free/Corbis; p. 19: © Reuters/CORBIS; p. 20: Derek P. Redfearn/The Image Bank/Getty Images; p. 22: © Royalty-Free/Corbis; p. 24: Digital Vision/Getty Images; p. 26: Nabil John Elderkin/Stone +/Getty Images

For information contact:

MONDO Publishing
980 Avenue of the Americas
New York, NY 10018

Visit our website at www.mondopub.com

Printed in China

08 09 10 11   9 8 7 6 5 4 3 2

ISBN 1-59336-768-6

Designed by Witz End Design

Contents

WHY I'D RATHER HAVE A JURY. . .

Your new substitute teacher leaves the room, and when she returns, she notices that something on her desk is missing. She accuses you of stealing it and says you can stand trial for the crime. You can be tried by a judge, who will be a principal from another school, or by a jury of your peers—which means twelve other kids from another school. Who would you choose?

Guess which kid the others will accuse of stealing something from the teacher's desk!

If it were me, I'd choose the twelve other kids. There are many reasons why I'd rather have my peers make this decision. Kids know what it's like to be a kid in a classroom. They realize a substitute teacher doesn't know the students as well as their own teacher and that often, because a substitute is trying to keep control, he or she can be unduly harsh. A principal might be quick to take a substitute teacher's side to enforce the substitute teacher's authority. But is this justice? I think a jury of peers—other kids—would do a better job determining the truth.

Before we talk more about why a jury is better than a judge, we need to understand a little about our court system. In America, people are "innocent until proven guilty." This means that the court has to prove that the defendant committed the crime. The lawyer who has to do this is called the prosecutor and has what's called the burden of proof—the job to prove to the court that the defendant is guilty under the law.

Anyone who commits a crime has the right to a trial. That person is called the defendant. Every defendant has a right to an attorney. If a person can't afford to hire a lawyer—and lawyers can be expensive—the court will appoint one, called a public defender, for free.

In our court system, there are two kinds of trials. A trial held before a judge is called a bench trial. The judge (who sits at a bench, or big desk) will hear testimony from the public defender or the defendant's attorney, as well as from the prosecutor, then the judge makes a decision based on the law.

If you go before a group of your peers, it's called a jury trial. While a bench trial is heard by a judge who knows and interprets the law, a jury trial means a person is judged by regular people, much like yourself. Juries listen to the facts and try to figure out what happened, but they don't have to know the law the way a judge does.

In most criminal cases, a jury is made up of twelve people. Individuals are chosen at random from voting records, and then must come to court on a certain day for jury selection. When their names are called, they might be asked to sit on a trial immediately. Or sometimes attorneys will ask questions to see if they would make good jurors. For instance, if the case was about a car accident, a lawyer might ask potential jurors if they were ever in a car accident because their experience may prejudice them against the defendant. If any juror knows a person who is on trial, he or she won't be allowed to serve on that trial because it wouldn't be fair.

Different states have different rules about whether a case goes before a judge or jury. Sometimes juries don't hear cases about traffic tickets, for example, but they do hear cases that have to do with injury, slander, and libel (spreading harmful lies), or breach of contract (making a written commitment to do something, then not doing it).

The United States Constitution gives us the right to a jury trial. If you want a jury trial but the other party does not, you're entitled to a jury trial because that is your right by law.

So, why would you want a trial by jury instead of a bench trial? Let's examine the facts.

Argument 1

Jury members work together with the objective of arriving at the correct decision. A judge doesn't have the advantage of discussing the case with others.

A jury lets people deliberate, or fully discuss an issue from many different sides, because there are many different personalities involved. Do you remember the phrase, "two heads are better than one"? Well, 12 heads are at work here, all determined to come to the best decision for a given case.

There is a famous movie called *Twelve Angry Men*. At the beginning of the movie, 11 of the jurors think a boy is guilty of killing his father in a domestic dispute, and only one man thinks he is innocent. Throughout the movie, the lone juror works to convince the other jurors of the boy's innocence. This movie is fascinating because it shows the power of persuasion. If you were innocent and all but one person thought you were guilty, wouldn't you want that individual trying to convince the other jurors of your innocence?

Production still from the movie *Twelve Angry Men*

The system works to make sure the jury is impartial. You can't be as sure with a judge.

A jury is meant to be composed of impartial individuals. To make sure of this, the lawyers on both sides of a case can remove any jurors who seem to be biased. Juries, because of the mix of individuals, also reflect the community as a whole. Can you say that about a judge, who is one individual with personal biases?

Jurors are not supposed to know the person they are judging, which is interesting considering the origins of the jury system. Back in the 11th century, jurors were chosen specifically because they knew the accused—someone who lived in the same neighborhood. Knowing the individual, jurors could determine who usually told the truth and who didn't. Could it be that the jury system was changed to the way it is today because it was discovered that knowing the defendant was not a good thing—and actually did not lead to justice?

Nowadays, potential jurors who are called to serve on a jury have to fill out a questionnaire that can be several pages long. Some questions don't seem to be relevant to the trial, like naming a favorite book or movie, but lawyers know that someone who goes to a lot of bloody horror movies, for example, might be less likely to flinch at a bloody trial.

Even if each member of the jury is not totally impartial, there are still 12 people, which is a built-in "checks and balances" system to avoid errors in the final decision. Would you want to take a chance with a judge, who is just one person?

Potential jurors must fill out questionnaires to determine their suitability.

7

With a jury, there can be more control. If you have been accused of a crime, you or your lawyer may be asked to help select the jury.

Knowing that you may be able to help select the jury may reassure you that you are likely to be judged by a jury of your peers, or people like yourself.

Although judges are supposed to be impartial, you can't know how they'll decide on your case. Even if you suspect that a particular judge may decide against you, there's nothing you can do personally to have the judge removed.

Potential jurors, however, can be questioned by attorneys to determine whether or not they might be sympathetic to your situation. Your lawyer can challenge a juror—or you can suggest that your lawyer challenge a juror—who appears biased and call for that individual to be excused. For example, a juror who looks at the defendant and blurts, "Only a guilty person would have a tattoo like that guy does!" is clearly not impartial. There's a good chance that someone who's acquainted with the defendant won't be impartial either. Both of these potential jurors would be challenged. This is a terrific way to make sure that the people who have input in your case are really going to be fair.

Some cases even employ a psychologist to help lawyers select the best jury possible. These psychologists can develop profiles of potential jurors, and these profiles might be useful for lawyers to select people they feel can be most impartial.

This lawyer is questioning a potential juror.

A jury can work around unfair laws.

Some laws are either old or outdated and need to be changed, or they are simply unfair. Or they may be laws that are indeed fair, such as not having or using a gun, but during an extraordinary circumstance those laws may need to be broken. For example, several years ago in Illinois, a gas station attendant who believed he was about to be killed used a gun to defend himself against a vicious robbery. Handguns were illegal in that part of Illinois, though, and the prosecutor wanted to send the gas station attendant to jail for owning and using one. Did the gas station attendant do the wrong thing? The jury acquitted him because it was clearly an issue of self-defense, and they felt it would be unjust to punish him for disobeying this law.

Sometimes juries are less concerned than judges with following a law exactly. Instead, they take into account how justice would best be served.

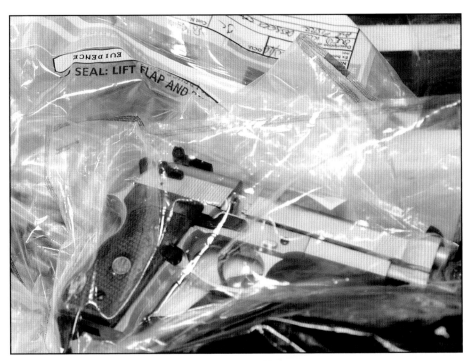

A gun that has been tagged as evidence

Jurors might be more sympathetic than a judge because they may follow their feelings rather than strictly following the law.

While the objective of a trial is to identify the truth, sometimes the personal feelings of a jury might help to bring about justice. For example, let's say there's a case where the defendant was accused of hurting a child. Potential jurors are probably asked if they have children of their own, a close relationship with children, or whether they feel people who hurt children should be automatically imprisoned. Those jurors who have children or feel strongly about punishing people who hurt children would probably be excused from serving. (This might not help the defendant out much, however, since most people feel strongly that children should be safe.) Imagine that the police broke into a person's apartment and found evidence linking that person to a crime against a child. Because there was no search warrant, the evidence can't be considered. But because the crime is so awful, it may be extremely difficult for jurors to put aside their personal feelings about children. This is a good thing because they might

The evidence that this lawyer is holding up may or may not be admissible.

work harder to find legitimate reasons to convict the accused than a judge who is trained to be impartial and strictly follow the law.

Or suppose a young person was accused of robbery. Under the law, a 15-year-old who steals some soda from a store may be legally guilty of robbery. But jurors might feel that since she is still a young person and the item was just a can of soda, she deserves a second chance and the benefit of the doubt. They might think that just the fact of being on trial might frighten her into never again leaving a store without paying.

Sometimes a juror acts on strong personal feelings rather than exclusively considering the facts of the case. But is this always a bad thing? Though courts want and need to stick to the facts, sometimes those feelings can make for a fairer decision.

Jurors, unlike many judges, have all the time they need to make a decision.

Jurors know how important it is to do a good job and what a privilege it is to be a part of our legislative process. Jurors know that someone else's life and livelihood are in their hands, and they take that very seriously.

Judges are used to being on the bench and may not pay the same kind of attention that jurors would. And judges are really busy—their court schedules are often so overcrowded that they don't have enough time to look at every aspect of a case. Judges may want to look at the facts of the case and come to a fair decision as soon as possible, so they can move onto the next one. Jurors are encouraged to take all the time they need and can deliberate for as long as necessary.

A jury foreman speaks to his fellow jury members before they begin their deliberations.

For example, when Charles Lindbergh's baby was kidnapped, the trial lasted five weeks. The jury had plenty of time to hear all the evidence and come to a decision. They did not have to worry about other cases getting delayed. They just had to think about the facts of the case in front of them.

Argument 7

A judge is just one person, and he or she can have biases.

Judges are supposed to be impartial, but they vary in the way that they interpret the law and in how they might rule on a particular case. Some judges have conservative positions, while others take more open or liberal views.

That's why there are so many disagreements about judges who are nominated by the President of the United States to join our Supreme Court. Often there are great political battles over a Supreme Court nomination. Senators want to get a good idea of how a particular judge sees the law and interprets the Constitution before putting that person on the Supreme Court bench.

Justices of the United States Supreme Court in 2006

For example, let's look at the way two judges might determine the meaning of freedom of speech. Under the Constitution, all people have the right to freedom of speech. Consider the example of wearing a T-shirt to school with writing on it. Is it legal for your teacher to send you home to change, claiming that all that writing is distracting and not appropriate clothing for school? A conservative judge might say it is, because you are under the rule of the school. A more liberal judge might say it isn't, because you have freedom of speech under the Constitution. But you can't choose the judge you want for a trial. Judges are always appointed, so you never know what kind of judge you might get.

Also, any illness, conflict, or distraction is bound to affect one individual more than it would affect an entire group. One juror being sick or unfocused for several days wouldn't affect the other members of the jury, and thus wouldn't greatly affect the jury's decision. But if the judge who is deciding your case isn't feeling well or is going through a difficult time, that would have a great impact because he or she is the only one responsible for the decision. In addition, a judge may have a personal prejudice against you or your attorney or may be thinking of other matters. He or she also may have just dealt with a problematic case similar to yours, and the judgment may be colored by that experience.

Judges may use your case as a test case to change a law they don't like.

Have you heard the term "activist judge"? That means a judge who is trying to make law instead of just interpreting it. Such judges can ignore the meaning of the Constitution to invent new rights, using their moral opinions instead of their legal knowledge.

For example, in one recent case, Judge Roy Moore displayed a monument of the Ten Commandments in a public place despite the Constitution's clear stand on a dividing line between church and state.

He ignored a federal judge's order to remove it, causing the judge to declare that Moore "placed himself above the law." Moore was then removed from office. It seems clear that Moore wanted to make this a test case to blur the lines separating church and state.

Whether you agree with Moore's position on this issue or not, is it right for any one person to decide that he or she is above the law—especially that of the Constitution?

While judges may be trying to change the law using a particular case, a jury is only interested in the case itself. A jury can't change laws, so all their attention is focused on the specifics of the case. A judge may be interested in the case only because it represents an opportunity to change the law.

The shadow of a man praying looms over the Ten Commandments monument at the Alabama Judical Building.

There are unethical judges, or those who show poor judgment.

While some jurors don't take their duty seriously, it's rare for more than a few members to be problematic. Incompetent or unethical judges, however, do exist, and it's much more difficult to get them off a case. One poor decision from a judge can ruin a person's life. There are cases where a judge has decided, for example, that a woman who is beaten by her husband is not allowed protection under the law. Then the husband has future opportunities to hurt or even kill her. Some judges make disparaging remarks to defendants about the way they look or choose to dress, or in general make it clear that they feel the defendant is guilty before being tried! Some judges are even criminals, taking bribes to insure an innocent verdict.

How can the system get rid of incompetent judges? It isn't easy. Lawyers don't often want to risk exposing a bad judge, especially if the lawyer has to appear before that same judge on another occasion. A corrupt judge can hold grudges against lawyers, making them lose a case or even ruin their practice. To remove a judge, charges have to be brought before a board and the board has to consider whether or not to disbar, or remove, the judge.

Former Federal Judge Martin T. Manton (right) shown arriving at Federal Court in June, 1939. He was sentenced to two years in prison and fined $10,000 for selling his decisions while on the bench.

Judges are often slow in giving their decisions.

Imagine you've been caught staying out past your curfew, and you know your parents are going to punish you. Would you rather find out your punishment now or wait until morning? It can be very frustrating not knowing what's going to happen to you.

Judges can delay decisions for months. Sometimes judges put off their decisions simply because they are backlogged with other cases—they haven't had enough time to properly review the case and consider what would be the best thing to do. Other times judges plan to review the case at a later date, perhaps when they return from a vacation or a conference. But if you are the person going on trial, wouldn't you want justice to be served as swiftly as possible?

How long will it take until this judge has the time to review your case?

17

Argument 11

A judge is only one person making the decision instead of 12 people.

Would you want only one person deciding what will happen in your case? A judge finds the facts in the case and has to interpret those facts. The interpretation of the facts then determines the outcome. If the judge thinks you are guilty, then you are found guilty. If the judge thinks you are innocent, then you are innocent. Having 12 people is a safeguard. The defendant is better protected because it's more difficult for 12 people to come to one decision about the case than it is for one person. Twelve people spend time discussing—and possibly disagreeing—giving them the opportunity to arrive at a fair decision. The defendant isn't at the mercy of one person's opinion. Wouldn't you rather have a majority opinion than the decision of only one person?

Jurors being sworn in. They may take an oath on a religious book of their choice or by making a faith-neutral affirmation.

Judges are trained not to let emotions get in their way, but sometimes emotions are helpful in making decisions.

It is not commonly known, but defense attorneys rarely want a judge trial because a jury is more likely to feel sympathy for the defendant and give that person the benefit of the doubt. Clearly a lawyer believes emotions can be useful in certain cases. There is nothing wrong with emotions playing a part in helping a jury to seek justice. For instance, if you were on a jury hearing a case of a drunk driver who killed people, wouldn't your emotions help you come up with the proper verdict?

Some people believe that judges are better than juries because they are trained to ignore inadmissible evidence. But isn't it true that in some cases emotions are important, and perhaps even necessary?

This stoic judge will not let emotions sway
her as she works toward making a decision.

Conclusion

We'd rather have a jury!

It's better to let 12 of your peers decide. A judge is just one person. A jury is less biased and more likely to look for a fair solution. Juries often decide more quickly and are more likely to rule against harsh laws.

Is It Better to be Judged by a Jury of Your Peers Than by a Judge?

Glossary

acquit
to find a person not guilty

assault
an attempt to physically injure another

attorney
a lawyer

bench trial
a trial where the case goes before a judge

breach of contract
when someone has signed a paper saying he or she will do something, and then doesn't do it

burden of proof
the prosecutor's job to prove to the court that the defendant is guilty under the law

cause
a reason to dismiss or excuse a potential juror

challenge
to object to a potential juror

checks and balances
the system where each branch of an organization can limit the power of another branch (usually refers to balancing the power of the executive, judicial, and legislative branches of the government)

defendant
the person charged with the crime

deliberating
the act of a jury discussing the case and coming to a decision about it

evidence
see: legal evidence

hearsay
the passing along of information told by someone else

hung jury
a jury that is unable to come to a decision and agree on a verdict. This results in a mistrial.

inadmissible evidence
evidence that cannot be used

"innocent until proven guilty"
a phrase that means a defendant is considered innocent until the court can prove guilt of a crime

jury trial
a trial where the case goes before a jury

legal evidence
proof that a specific event occured

libel
the spreading of harmful lies about someone else—in writing

mistrial
a trial that becomes invalid; for example, one in which the jurors cannot agree on a verdict

plaintiff
the party who initiates a lawsuit by filing a complaint against the defendant

prosecutor
a lawyer who attempts to prove the defendant guilty

public defender
a court-appointed lawyer for defendants who can't afford to hire one

reasonable doubt
the level of certainty a juror must have in order to find a defendant guilty of a crime

safeguard
something that insures safety

search warrant
a legal document required in order to search a person's home to find evidence

sequester
to place in isolation

slander
the spreading of harmful lies about someone else—in speech

verdict
the findings of a jury in a trial

walk
to go free because there's not enough evidence determining guilt